The children were at school. It was playtime.

"Come in," called Mrs May.

Mrs May told the children a story. The story was about a village. The village was in the mountains.

Everyone liked the story. It was called The Village in the Snow.

The children went to Biff's room. They wanted an adventure.

Biff picked up the magic key. The key began to glow.
"The magic is working," said Biff.

The magic took the children to the village in the snow.
“It’s lovely,” said Biff.

Kipper jumped in the snow.
"I like the snow," he called. "This is fun."

They played in the snow. They made a snowman and put Kipper's hat on top.

They jumped in the snow. They threw snowballs.

“Look,” said Wilma.

They saw a little boy. The boy was pulling a toboggan. Some big boys ran up.

They pushed the little boy over. They pushed the toboggan over and they ran away.

The children ran up. They helped the little boy. Kipper picked up his hat.

The little boy told them about the big boys. Kipper was cross.

Kipper put on the little boy's hat. He put on his coat.
"Come on," he called.

The big boys looked at Kipper.
Kipper looked like the little boy.
“Come on,” said the big boys.

The children threw snowballs at the big boys.
"Help! Help!" yelled the big boys.

The big boys ran away. The little boy jumped and jumped in the snow.

The children put the little boy on the toboggan. They pulled him home.

The little boy lived with his grandfather.

Grandfather gave the children a drink. The children told Grandfather about the big boys.

They told Grandfather about the snowball fight.

The children played in the snow. They went on the toboggan.

"This is fun," said Wilf.

The magic key began to glow.
“It’s time to go,” said Biff. “Come on,”
she said.

The magic took the children home.
"What an adventure!" said Chip.